"In *Fountain of Grace*, Gayle Schrank shares the fruit of her reflection in an engaging, beautiful way. Gayle's years as a lay ecclesial minister and dedicated disciple of Jesus Christ are evident in her poetry. As food for thought and prayer, *Fountain of Grace: Encounters with God* provides great opportunities to ponder our Lord's love, mercy and many blessings."
— Most Reverend Charles C. Thompson
Archbishop of Indianapolis

+++

+ + +

Foreword

We each have been given a beautiful life to live, and when we turn to God with all our joys and sorrows, He will magnify our joy, carry our sorrows, and enlarge our hearts, so His glory can be made known.

God made each of us to be a beautiful fountain of His grace. It is through our life's experiences we are carved and molded into these vessels in which God's radiance is revealed. Our life here on earth is a journey of discovery. Our unique purpose and the grace offered to us during our lifetime is a personal gift we receive from our Creator. God assures us His all-powerful and never-ending gift of grace is always dependable and sufficient.

At our Baptism, God fills our soul with His grace. Through this grace we grow in hope, and receive light for the empty recesses of our souls. When the darkness from the emptiness tries to dominate our lives, it is through prayer that God's grace pours forth and overflows into those dark places.

Through our prayers and listening God will transform our darkness into light and our doubt into trust. With prayer, words are not needed. Resting in God's presence is enough. With His grace we are freed to be our best selves, and it is in those moments our heart is united with Christ and we become His beautiful fountain of grace.

The person you are, your truest self, cannot be seen or touched. It can only be loved. May that be our desire – to love one another. God's grace is ever-present to us through prayer, so let us not limit ourselves.

Together, as we pray and seek God's grace, let us lift ourselves and one another up to God. He will show us the goodness and beauty that lives within our hearts. As I am writing this I am praying for you and I ask you to please include me in your prayers. Always remember God knows all your needs. His grace is always there for you, and he made you to be a fountain of His grace.

"My grace is sufficient for you, for power is made perfect in weakness.
I will rather boast most gladly of my weaknesses,
in order that the power of Christ may dwell with me."
2 Corinthians 12:9

1

+ + +

+ + +

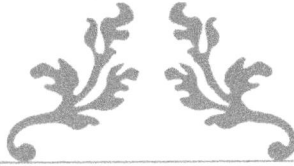

Fountain of Grace

Encounters with God

Gayle Schrank

2020
Home Crafted Artistry & Printing
Lanesville, Indiana

+ + +

This publication is intended to be poetic representations in regard to the subject matters covered. All poems here presented are the author's original work. The statements and opinions expressed in this book are those of the author. Any resemblance to specific people or events not specifically named are coincidental and are not intended, except that capitalized pronouns not usually capitalized in standard usage refer to God.

ISBN: 978-1-7323437-6-4

Published 2020 by Home Crafted Artistry & Printing with permission of the author.

Home Crafted Artistry & Printing
2404 Scenic Drive NE #6
Lanesville, IN 47136
website: www.HomeCraftedArtstry.com
e-mail: HomeCraftedArtistry@yahoo.com

Cover design by Gayle Schrank and Mary Bibb Smith
Photos property of Gayle Schrank.
Proudly printed in the United States of America.

+ + +

For my grandchildren.

*I am so thankful for the innocence and love you share with me.
You are a true gift from God!*

Thank you Lord for making us a family.

+ + +

+ + +

Preface

I have spent many hours with God in conversation. I have taken into my heart the prayers and needs of myself and others, and I seek God and His grace in those places. These writings are the result of those encounters with God.

Some of my prayers are the same, or similar, and titled with different names...pay attention. When we open our heart and invite God inside, His unchanging and gentle love will reach the divisions within us, so we can recognize ourselves more honestly.

God loves each of us so perfectly, and when we are able to listen to God, it is in those moments His grace is most abundant and overflowing, and we know our prayers are being heard.

As you read these pages, I pray for God's grace to surround you. I pray for His goodness to increase in you. But mostly, I pray for you to know and receive more fully God's abundant love for you personally.

When we love ourselves and one another with God's perfect love, our lives are filled and overflowing with His grace and peace.

It is in those moments we encounter God!

+ + +

Contents

Part One: **Poems** *(in alphabetical order)*

+ + +

+ + +

+ + +

Part Two: **Christmas Poems** *(in year order)*

+ + +

A

A Mother's Heart

Mary's love is an arc of God's grace,
Rising above waves of injustice and hate.
With a mother's heart that belongs to Christ,
She protects and guards through evil and plight.

Mary teaches us to always act as we should.
She will mold us as Jesus, to be humble and good.
Do not turn away from her friendship and love.
She will lift us to Christ, who reigns up above.

Our eternal souls will not stay here on earth.
When our bodies die, there will be a rebirth.
Mary's love will help us never to fear.
She knows Christ the immortal is always near.

As Jesus' mother, she is our mother too.
Her hand is reaching out and waiting for you.

All Are One

Our emotions and the depth
Of what we feel will help form us
Into the person we become.
Let us call to mind
Every breath is
Praise to our God,
Through whom all are one.

All Are Searching

Lord, help us listen to one another.
We have to stop hearing others say,
"You're wrong!"
You know all are searching
For the meaning of life.
We want to discover where we belong.
Our words can be so inadequate.
So often their meanings we try to control.
Heavenly Father, only your Love is complete.
Unite our hearts, Lord, please make us whole.

May we listen today with the ear of our heart!

Are We Truly Free?

As Jesus waits patiently
For each of us to seek and find Him,
Mary, His constant advocate (and ours)
Guards us with a Mother's love.
She upholds us,
As any mother does her child,
And pleads we hold our Brother's hand.
When we listen and obey,
Our hearts are satisfied.
And in that moment,
We truly know and love our Father,
And ourselves.
Only then,
Are we truly free!

Authentic Love

The genuine and loving person God made you to be
Desires to be known and longs to be free

Your journey of life will take you
In so many directions
Don't get carried away
With your own desires and affections

God is reaching for you with each breath you take
Do you turn away with doubts and unwisely forsake

Discover God's great love for you
So your authentic love can grow
God's faithfulness will open your heart
And all goodness you will know

B

Battle the Darkness Within

The time is getting closer,
And elections are drawing near.
Be still and pay attention,
Or that small voice we will not hear.
Before we oppose one another,
We must first
Battle the darkness within.
Call to mind Jesus' love is perfect,
And we don't want to battle with him.

Be at Rest

Lord, help me know how to be my best.
May I be filled with you and be at rest.
The choices that I make each day,
Will unite or divide, so I ponder and pray.

Be Grateful

Heavenly Father
I will rest in your hands
Please fill my heart
With Your divine plan
As I sit and wonder
As I breathe and remain
You fill me with goodness
You remove my pain
I will forever
Be grateful to you
Help me Lord
Be true to you

Be Renewed

Lord, help me rise up
And face those dark places within.
It is your kindness and grace
That give me strength to begin.
May the weariness of my day
Become a prayer to you.
It is only by your mercy, Lord,
I can hope to be renewed
Amen.

+ + +

Be Sincere

Lord I want to be sincere.
It is not hard to do until my doubting heart rears.
What a shame it is how I judge myself.
I must not compare my life with anyone else.

Lord help me recognize the gifts I have been given.
To improve myself I will look to you
And to the heavens.

My life is meant to live
With purpose and for service.
That will not happen if my daily living
Exists on the surface.

I want to be better at being who you made me to be.
What I think, say, and do, will bind my heart
Or set me free.

Lord your perfect love always provides what I need.
You love each of us the same
So I will be sincere and be just me.

Be Steadfast

Lord, convict our hearts today
Help us want what is good
Give us courage to be steadfast
And pursue the things we should

As we wonder, dream and hope
Keep us rooted in your truth
May the desires we pursue
Draw us closer to you.

+ + +

Be Still

There is a hunger for wholeness
That only God can give.
And so we must not legislate how to love and live.

When government tries to rule
What belongs to God,
We diminish our ability to follow where Christ trod.

Within our souls is where He lives.
Be still and take heed.
Or we will be left wanting.
For it is God who fills our needs.

Bring Peace to the World

When you find yourself among conflict,
Are you able to give your best?
Or do you avoid, get angry and defensive.
Through what means does your heart find rest?

Our honest answer to this question
Is a good measure to help us know.
Am I helping to bring peace to the world,
Or am I enabling division to grow?

Broken Praise

Lord, when I am bound by life,
And my daily living becomes a chore,
I call on you with confidence.
You give comfort and so much more.

So with your help, my humble God,
I will rest in you this day.
Your peace gives healing and wholeness to all,
And so I offer my broken praise.

C

Call on God

The whole world deserves our prayers.
Our love alone is not enough.
May we humble ourselves and bow before God.
His Divine Love will increase in us.

All of God's creation is in need.
The paradox of living confuses and divides.
Our daily contradictions in each of our lives
Injures our hearts and causes false pride.

It is difficult to not dwell on feelings.
But, our emotions must not persuade.
It is our prayers that call on God.
He will restore hearts and provide needed aid.

Don't compromise your integrity.
Always commit to doing what is right.
Be steadfast and take delight in God.
He will pour forth His power and might.

+ + +

Call Out His Name

All souls are united
Through a God we cannot see
His Love pours out
To all the world
Freely given to you and me

Your soul knows His goodness
You were fashioned then set free
God longs for your return
Friendship with God is meant to be

When you are seeking fulfillment
Listen for His voice
Call out his name
In the silence
You will find Him
You will never be the same

Carry Me

There is so much to do and yet I wait.
Why is it, Lord, I hesitate?
Come Holy Spirit, help me do what I ought.
Give wisdom and counsel to my wondering heart.

The needs are many, so I turn to you.
Remove the distractions that want to confuse.
Lord, hold my hand and open my mind.
So often I feel helpless and blind.

Show me your beauty and help me to know.
Your Way is imprinted within my soul.
Truth will remove all darkness and fear.
Your Love assures us that Light is near.

So whether sitting or serving others;
In prayer I lift up my sisters and brothers.
Help me Lord, to always see you.
When I falter, your mercy will carry me through.

+ + +

Choose Goodness

Freedom is something we so often take for granted,
And it shapes the full person we become.
Our free will gives us the power to make choices.
We must choose goodness to be a unified one.

Communion

What am I attached to?
What is keeping me from growing?
I am holding onto something.
So, I turn to God who is all knowing.

Lord, the talents you bestow to us
Will not merit your good pleasure,
When we fail to seek your friendship
And live by our own measures.

Help me embrace you today.
May your love live in my faith.
May your glory always surround me.
Your Communion steeps us in grace.

Created In His Image

God's truth is such a beautiful thing,
Our fulfillment it will bestow.
It was put in place when the world began,
And its meaning we must seek to know.

God created each of us perfectly.
We are created in His image.
He set us free when He formed our souls,
And our life is but a pilgrimage.

The mystery of our God
Is a topic to learn and discuss,
For the significance of our days
Is determined by Him not us.

Although we do not understand
We mustn't be afraid.
God's love is all embracing
And He forgives when we betray.

His mercy will always reveal to us
The errors of our ways.
His love and grace surround us
Especially when we pray.

Christ's Spirit will always reveal to us
How He is the giver of life.
And when we turn to Him in love
He gives His peace for our strife.

Ask yourself, "Do I know Him?
Do I truly know the Lord of Life?"
He deserves the very best of you.
For YOU he paid the price.

So, delight in Christ and claim big things
And remember He's your Creator.
In return He will give you His joy-
Today, tomorrow, forever.

D

Daily Contradictions

The whole world deserves your prayers.
Our love alone is not enough.

May we humble ourselves and bow before God.
His Divine Life will increase in us.

God's creations are all in need.
The paradox of life will confuse and divide.

These daily contradictions in each of our lives
Wound our hearts and produce false pride.

It is difficult to not dwell on feelings.
But, our emotions must not persuade.

It is in our prayers that we call on God.
He restores hearts and will give needed aid.

Don't compromise your honor.
Always commit to doing what is right.

Be steadfast and take delight in God.
He will pour forth His power and might.

Darkness and Its Power

Darkness, which belongs to evil, tries to hide the truth and will enable
or encourage uncertainty and illusion – and it is carried out by people.
If it is my calling to act against this darkness, then I must humbly
surrender myself to God.

Knowing that the darkness and its power wish to engulf me, I must
put my hope in God so my sorrow and anguish will become a prayer
of enlightenment and forgiveness.

Dawn of How

We cannot achieve today
The things meant for tomorrow.
Time and lessons that are needed
Are impossible to borrow.

This moment is your gift.
Devote yourself to now.
Embrace what you've been given,
For it is the dawn of how.

How will tomorrow be?
That we do not know.
But the seeds we sow today
Help us know that we will grow.

Growth brings wisdom and guarantees
We have all that we need.
Life is precious so be thankful,
The dawn of how is now, indeed.

Diverse and Free

This time in history is meant for you and me.
When we are divided,
We chance our justice and liberty.

The complex webs we weave
Can bring good or ill to our lives.
When we deceive and manipulate
Its effect will trigger strife.

Embracing one another will enable us to see
The goodness that brings peace and sincere fidelity.
Being an American means we are diverse and free.
If we don't protect what we have,
We will lose our autonomy.

+ + +

Divine Direction

Lord, take my distractions,
And turn them into prayers.
I know your love and charity
Are with me everywhere.

God, I call to you Most High,
To protect when life engulfs me.
I trust you will pour unto me
Divine direction and great mercy.

Divine Goodness

God's Divine Goodness given to you,
Is meant for you alone.
This gift given to the world through you,
Needs your "yes" to find its home.

Those who seek faith will discover it.
Though invisible it's easily found.
We live and breathe this love each day.
Yet for many it still confounds.

Look within – you will find it.
God is waiting to be embraced.
That yearning to love, and be loved;
Its Divine Goodness, and your choice to make.

+ + +

Don't Be Afraid

That Divine Goodness
We each have inside
Is humble yet all-powerful
We are diverted by our pride

Do you know the person
God summoned you to be?
Are you listening?
Do you care?
It is God's Love that sets us free

The paradox of daily living
Causes many to lose their way
Make a promise to pay attention
Follow Christ
Don't be afraid

We all are searching
We get hurt and harden our hearts
Listen and take notice
Now is a good time to start

Spend some time with God today
Be still and breathe His peace
Christ helps us carry our burdens
And He provides for every need

COME FOLLOW ME!

+ + +
DON"T LOSE HOPE

If you and another person are in opposition with each other, you are in good company; our world is filled with discontent. Even Jesus' disciples did not always see eye to eye. However, as children of God we are called to a higher standard. Now, replace your name with Peter's or Paul's, and grow in knowledge of Christ's love for all.

Peter said to Paul one day…
"I wish you were not here.
Your transgressions have appalled me,
And I do not want you near."

Then Jesus reminded Peter,
"Paul has many gifts to give.
His sins have been forgiven,
And his life he now must live.

I have given Paul a purpose
That you can't take away.
Although it may be difficult,
I am asking Paul to stay.

You may not like one another.
That itself is not a sin.
But, if you cannot act in love,
That's where the sin begins.

So, Peter, please be kind now,
I have given you work too.
Your life was set with meaning,
And you have a job to do.

My gift of courage is here for you.
Please give your pride to me.
Your weakness I will take from you,
So your heart can be set free.

I ask you now, come walk with me.
My children, I love you both.
Never forget my promise.
I am with you.
Don't lose hope."

"Be kind to one another, compassionate, forgiving one another as God has forgiven you in Christ."
Ephesians 4:32

Doubt

Be careful of your unbelief.
It will rob you of your life.
Taking from your heart what's real,
Doubt replaces Love with strife.

E

Eternal Love

The goodness we each have inside
Was given by our Lord
And so it is our Creator
Whom we should praise and adore

When Christ calls us we should listen
That is the true meaning of obey
Our hearts will then be opened
And His eternal love will forever stay

Every Life Matters

Every life matters.
Black and white alike.
Police officers and civilians.
We must not fill our life with strife.

Old people, young people;
Unborn babies too.
Every life matters.
Because God made me and you.

F

Find Peace

We find peace by finding God.
For we know conflicts are everywhere.
God's Divine Goodness dwells within us.
Where there is unrest God is already there.

Know God, know peace...no God, no peace.

+ + +

Freedom

We are American; we are diverse;
We are strong; we are free.
Do we really know what that means?
Our freedom we defend is a God-given gift.
God's goodness will help us to see.

The freedom we enjoy is something great…
It's far greater than freedom itself.
We hold up our flag to let the world see,
With freedom we have much wealth.

Abundance of opportunity, liberty and land…
These gifts are given to unite.
The prosperity we have is given for all.
These things were not meant to start fights.

God's gift of freedom dwells within…
And no one can take it away.
When Christ was born into this world,
God's freedom was here to stay.

God's freedom overcomes oppression!
Freedom's love conquers false pride!
This freedom was born through Jesus!
All fears freedom does subside!

As a nation we stand, but through God all are one.
Freedom knows no separation.
We must join together with freedom and faith.
And thank God for His great creation.

Each day of the year let us remember with joy,
True freedom was born through Mary, as a boy.
Christ's freedom was given for you and for me;
To uphold and to share…
May the whole world be free!

+ + +

Fullness of Life

The goodness we were created for
Is something we ought not deny.
Sometimes we may want things done our way.
Yet, God's perfection we should not defy.

God wills for us a love that is one,
With no divisions, just fullness of life.
We must call to mind, our love is disordered,
And along with it comes chaos and strife.

If we want peace and love that endures,
We must seek and follow Christ's path.
Together, let us seek faith, hope, and love.
May we find God's truth that will last.

G

Give Our Best

When each of us has overcome,
God's promise is at rest,
And on those days we struggle,
We must carry on
And give our best.

In time all blessings will unfold,
For God never leaves our side.
In our joys and all our sorrows,
His Spirit does always abide.

+ + +

God and His Grace

There's a Love far greater than your love and mine.
We are fools to turn away from this Love
That's Divine.

Its strength will give you courage.
Lasting courage comes from our faith.
You must seek to find this enduring gift.
Love poured out through God and His grace.

God Called Us

You deserve rights because you are you,
I deserve rights because I am me.
We all were given inalienable rights
When God called us to be.

God Is Calling

Faith is not a guarantee
Goodness is all around
Faith is our assurance
God's love can always be found

God resides within all hearts
Be still and look within
When hope seems lost
God is calling
His love in us is where faith begins

+ + +

God's Perfect and Unending Love

Each of us has been given the beautiful gift of life. We are personally fashioned by God Himself, and then set free. Our time in this world is a journey, and our life gives us opportunity to discover God's perfect and unending love. Our love is not yet perfected, so we search and discover together what God's love teaches, and how we are each called to live it out.

God is waiting for each of us, and Christ has restored us, so by the power of the Holy Spirit, may we embrace this great faith we have been given. Devoted with one accord, let us go out and tell the Good News to those we encounter each day, through our words, and most importantly through our actions…until that great day when we return to God.

{LOVE}
faith hope

Goodness Restored

Grace belongs to God.
It is showered down like rain.
The barriers we build around our heart,
Keep grace out and cause us pain.

Our prayers penetrate those obstacles,
And bring light in that place that is dark
If you want joy and goodness restored
Praying is a good place to start.

Grace Abounds

Are you preparing your heart to meet God
He is Omnipotent and there is no hiding
One day He will call you to Himself
Do you anticipate wrath or good tidings

Sit quietly and reflect with God today
No thoughts are too big or too small
Our being and wonders are given as gifts
God's grace abounds for one and all

Jesus gave us his Mother, Mary
When he was hanging from the cross
She will hold us as she did Jesus
When we are frightened, hurt, or lost

Her love is gentle and caring
Always directing our hearts to her Son
She will walk with us in our battles
Her extra graces were given for everyone

She said, "Yes" when this was asked of her
Through Jesus she is our Mother too
So I honor Mary in a special way
Today and all year through

Happy New Year

When Christ's hope controls our hearts,
God's peace is what we know.
May the New Year be filled with grace,
As God's goodness provides and love grows.

...KNOW YOU ARE LOVED

Happy Valentine's Day!

Lord, I need your help to do what is right.
Please remove from my heart
The darkness of sin and vice.

Your truth is all-telling
Yet we must seek to understand.
I trust in your love O Lord.
Walk with me and hold my hand.

For you alone are the Lord of Love.
Please guide my heart today.
What a fitting way to direct our prayers,
On this feast of Valentine's Day.

He Wills You

God's dwelling in the human heart
Is a sacred place indeed,
And, the Heart of hearts bids your loves,
So He can serve your needs.

He reaches down to lift you up,
And is waiting for your hand.
He never loses patience,
For love is His command.

Your Father mightily safeguards your soul,
But, the final choice belongs to you.
Remember, His Love is a holy treasure
He wills you…be faithful and be true!

+ + +

Healing and Grace

In our desire to help others,
We don't know where to begin.
We must be careful our wounded compassion,
Doesn't assist weakness or sin.

God knows our hearts.
He is not restricted to time or place.
In prayer let us join our hearts together.
God will send forth His healing and grace.

Heaven on Earth

When we do the right things for the right reasons,
We enable miracles to abound.
Desiring goodness for the benefit of others,
Is when Heaven on Earth can be found.

Heavenly Gifts

God's love for you is eternal
His heavenly gifts are forever proclaimed
His freedom will provide liberation for the world
Even if we are bound by chains

In truth we are animals by nature
Only by God does our love turn divine
We must seek friendship with our Creator and Lord
His heavenly gifts will be born in our lives

God's wisdom calls us to contemplate
He knows we are anxious and afraid
He wants to pour forth His heavenly gifts
We must remember in His image we are made

+ + +

His Goodness Remains

We mustn't become distracted,
Or forget the war has been won.
Animosity must never drive us,
Lest within us Christ's work is undone.

Let us turn to the Lord in prayer.
In you and me His goodness remains.
Christ conquered darkness once and for all.
Remember, His love is here to stay.

His Love

There are times in my life
When I feel weary.
I struggle and try
But can't seem to think clearly.

The happiness inside
Turns quickly to sorrow,
And I hope my tears
Become joy tomorrow.

My emotions are raw.
I feel gloomy and dim.
I may keep it hidden,
But there is pain within.

It is during these times
The Lord calls our names.
He wants to comfort
Because He knows our pain.

The Mighty Physician
Gives grace that heals.
He cures our afflictions
And woes that are real.

Our Lord has told us
He truly does care.
He won't force Himself on us.
That is why we have prayer.

We must turn to our God
With thanksgiving and praise.
He offers us hope,
Today and always.

Be still and listen
To the small voice inside.
The Lord is calling,
And He will help us abide.

Christ our Lord holds us close.
Our strength comes from above.
Let go and let God.
Receive the gift of His love.

+ + +

His Spirit Always Abides

When each of us has overcome,
God's promise is at rest.
On those days that we struggle,
We must carry on and give our best.

In time all blessings will unfold,
For God never leaves our side.
In our joys and all our sorrows,
His Spirit always abides.

Hold My Heart

There is a fear
In my heart
That I cannot name
I get mad
Then feel sad
And I want to blame

Help me
Lord Jesus
Hold my heart
Be my guide
With you
There is joy
Please stay by my side

Holy Spirit Come to Our Aid

Heaven was brought to earth
When Christ was born long ago.
Now our mission is to help others
So peace and goodness will grow.

Many souls are hurting.
Let us heed the cries of all.
Holy Spirit come to our aid!
Lift our hearts lest we fall.

Humble Power

Lord even in our darkest hours
You are providing for our needs.
Without You and Your abounding grace
We could not love, think or breath.

Some do not want Your friendship.
May one day they seek to see.
Your humble power gave us life.
Your goodness called our world to be.

I

I Come From Dust

I want to say, "Lord, send me!"
But, in myself I do not trust
Build me up in your divinity Lord
For I know I come from dust

If I must go I want to be ready
Because I want to follow you
Purify and cleanse me Lord
Through your mercy and grace
I will be true

I Need You

Why do we avoid our loneliness?
In that place I need you; you need me.
We must turn towards one another
God's love then descends
And fills our needs.

I Promise

I know you have a good heart.
Please know I do too.
Together we can be thoughtful
In our words and all we do.

I promise to care for and cherish
All that is true, noble and good.
Even when others may compromise
I will continue to act as I should.

I may not always feel happy
But together we can pave the way.
Our children and all the world will see,
We're stewards of peace.
It is here to stay.

Each of us is part of history.
Our great land is bursting with life.
The power of Love heals and unites.
Freed from darkness let's live in the Light.

+ + +

I Want What Is Good

Who is judging who?
We really cannot tell.
I can only know what is in my own heart.
Truth be told, I don't know that very well.

When my suffering heart yields for your well-being,
And it is for you that I want what is good,
Only then can I trust I am not judging
And I am acting as I should.

If Only...

If only we knew what we do not know,
We would take heed and awaken
God's love in our souls.

At odds with so many
We turn away and then we fret.
That does not solve our problems
Or resolve the world's regrets.
That place in our hearts reserved for Christ alone,
Was put there by God
So we could find our way home.

Nothing on earth is worth losing
Our conscience or one's self,
No reputation or position,
No profit, power or wealth.

When we think we are upright
But do not seek God's ways,
Our self-deception will take hold
Causing our hearts to go astray.
If only we knew what we do not know,
We would take heed and awaken
God's love in our souls.

+ + +

Ignite Your Light

One day peace will rule the land
Lawless violence will cease
Through God's abiding hand

As his vessels we are called
To lead and bring home
God's children – all people – exalted or forlorn

Lord I ask you to order my life
Please stay near me today and dissolve all strife

Release me from the criticism within
Ignite your light inside
Where lasting peace begins

In Him

We are each called
To gain victory
Over the negative forces
Within us,
That continually
Bring darkness
Into our lives.

Our will
Is what makes
This happen.
No person,
Or thing,
Can make
Those forces
Subside…

Only for a while
Can they take
Our mind
Off of that
Which lingers
In the shadows
Of our distractions.

The Spirit of God
Dwells with us now
And will lead us
Through this quest.

When we search
Our hearts,
We find Him there.
In Him
We discover
The light
And then rest.

44

In You I'll Abide

Those inclinations I possess;
They want to defy
God's holiness.

Lord, I surrender.
I am turning to you.
I repent and ask
For your virtues and truth.

Please be my light.
Cast the darkness aside.
Your love is my refuge.
In you I'll abide.

In Your Arms

Come into my heart Lord.
Please fill me with your praise.
The darkness of my soul,
Seems to never go away.

I need your love and mercy.
Without you I am blind.
Your will is what illuminates.
It is your wisdom that unbinds.

Hold me close to you, O Lord.
Pour out your love like gentle rain.
You are all that I desire.
In your arms there is no pain.

J

Join Hands

Just as children want their parents
All hearts yearn for the Divine
We have been separated from the One who made us
Our soul knows Him yet we remain blind

His peaceful Providence is calling
It reigns throughout the land
Lord, grant us joy and confidence in You
Only by your Love can we all join hands

K

Kindness and Grace

Our world needs more kindness and grace.
Sincerely offered its effect will disarm.
Kindness offers what is good.
Grace never wants to harm.

Help me Lord to trust in you.
Almighty God, please show me your face.
I know you will supply the means
You help me offer kindness and grace.

You magnify what is good.
You remove all my fears.
Lord, I call on you today.
Your friendship I hold dear.

Lord, pour forth your mercy.
Please help me to be humble.
Your kindness will impart reverence.
Your grace will help me not stumble.

L

Lasting Happiness

God is the author of reason.
He made what is absolute.
Slowly, we discover these hidden mysteries;
God's creations we cannot dispute.

These unseen truths we have come to know
First came from God not us.
Lord, help me unfold Your knowledge and logic.
Lead me to Your lasting happiness.

Lasting Peace

Happiness is short lived
When it is pleasure that we seek.
Loving and serving others
Is what creates joy and lasting peace.

+ + +

L E N T

What would you do,
If you were hungry,
And had no food to eat…

What would you do,
If you were cold,
And were living on the streets…

What would you do,
If you were afraid,
And had nothing to call your own…

What would you do?
That's a question to ask,
Those scared and all alone.

You are called
To help those in need,
But first you must open your heart.
God will show you how to assist,
And Lent is a good time to start.

Compassion and caring will help you begin,
To know what it is you should do.
The answers lie within each of us.
So tell me,
What will you do?

Let's Encounter Needs Together

+ + +

Let Us Pray

The Rosary helps me grow in prayer.
Mary's closeness with Jesus,
She so willingly shares.
She lifts my heart up to Christ.
It is He who heals my obsessions and vices.

Her intercession joins with mine.
She gives glory to God. He's the One Who's Divine
I need not fear Mary's mediation.
I will hold her hand without hesitation.

I do not worship Mary. She is my best friend.
She talks about Jesus, how strife He will mend.
I encourage you too, sit with Mary awhile.
Her Mother's Love brought Jesus smiles.

She gives comfort and sooths
Our suffering and grief
She knows it is Jesus Who offers relief.

So I will cry out my Rosary today.
I invite you to join me.
Let us pray…

Live Boldly

The expectations we have for others
Should be first lived in our own personal lives.
Baring pardon and justice let us live boldly,
Withholding all judgment and pride.

It sounds so simple yet it is hard to do.
But, I hope we are willing to try.
Remember, as water puts out fires,
Our good actions pour hope into our lives.

+ + +

Lord, Open Our Heart

Our world is so disordered.
We're stuck in the web
Of confusion and deceit.
It is Christ's love that will free us.
Despair and sadness His mercy defeats.

The weapons of love
Are the powers which save.
Lord open our heart
Help us see.
May we seek your forever glory,
And keep our eyes on eternity.

Love Abides

I refuse to race after
Those chasing the world.
I will only grow weary and tired.
Instead, I will cling to my God and Savior.
His Holy Spirit will always inspire.

I will not run,
Nor shall I hide;
For it's in Christ's peace
That love abides.

Love and Be Loved

Time is a means to measure our lives.
If we are honest many days we merely survive.
Our souls were made for so much more.
Let us love and be loved so our hearts will soar.

May your sorrows become compassion.
May your burdens subside to hope.
Pray! It brings our world mercy.
And we will thrive, not merely cope.

Love Can Grow

Lord, help me to seek what you desire,
And sincerely want what you want me to know.
May your goodness go before me always,
So my heart by your love can grow.

If I am to trust the desires of my heart,
Lord, I need your merciful grace.
I want to know, love, and serve what is good.
Please guide me today, Lord.
Show me your face.

Love From Above

There is a yearning in our hearts
That will always remain,
For in this world
We cannot attain

The perfection of love
We long to feel,
And in our soul
We know it is real;

The pure love of God
From where we came.
We grasp and we struggle,
And give it a name…

Success and fortune,
Good health and fame.
We chase after this love
And always in vain.

We must slow down.
God is here in this place.
He provides in good measure
Through His intimate grace.

He abides in our heart.
It is there He will teach
Of His personal love
That's within our reach.

Once found we must share
This wonderful love,
Because others are yearning
For this love from above.

+ + +

Loved Beyond Measure

Lord, in your embrace,
We are loved beyond measure,
And while living in this world
We will not be fully treasured.

Therefore, I must love others
The way that you love me.
We all want to know
We're cherished.
Through that we are set free.

Love's Command

Lord our world is filled with such mysteries
For the skies were formed by your hands
And all the created things in our universe
Come from your almighty love's command

The people who have gone before us
Help us know what we're called to do
You came into our world long ago
Preparing the way for our return to you

This journey we each are on
Gives us a personal glimpse of you
When we follow your light we find love
You give perspective and new points of view

Recalling those three kings on a journey
Like them we follow stars and find you
We will bring our gifts and give you homage
Bowing in reverence because we are made new

Your presence among us is important
Without you we are incomplete
Your fellowship with us in the Eucharist
Is where our souls and your love can meet

M

Majestic Love

When we reach out to our God in need,
His grace within our heart expands.
God shields our soul with His majestic love,
As we rest in His compassionate hands.

God's tender love will carry us.
Our fragile heart He will never break.
God protects us and restores our lives.
He provides our healing from harm and heartache.

Mary's Immaculate Heart

How could one say we don't need Mary?
That's like saying we don't need our legs.
We can reach Jesus quickly,
Or drag ourselves slowly instead.

I have discovered God's heavenly path.
She's filled with such beauty and favor.
As I follow Mary's immaculate heart,
God transforms my sorrows to pleasures.

"My soul proclaims the greatness of the Lord,
My spirit rejoices in God my Savior."
Luke 1:46-47

+ + +

Miracles

If we do the right things for the right reasons
We enable Miracles to abound.

Let us desire goodness for the sake of the world,
So heaven on earth can be found.

Moment by Moment

When I am able to trust in the Lord,
I know His love is without measure.
When I find myself holding back,
I want to seek God and what He treasures.

What is it that I am clinging to?
Is it comfort, leisure, doubt, or fear?
Whatever it is moment by moment,
I can be assured God's grace is near.

My Prayer for the Day

This journey I have called life
Is beautiful indeed
It will enlighten and empower
When I turn to God who sets me free

I desire to love
And be loved in return
Yet my poverty often obscures
The lessens I'm meant to learn

Help me Lord to listen
I lift my heart up to you
Show me the errors of my ways
I need your mercy and your truth

Amen

N

New Life

When you are lonely and in need of a friend
Remember the Holy Spirit is by your side
God will restore your joy and hope
He bestows love and peace of mind

God's ways are kind and gentle
His mystery is always within our reach
Let us seek God with our starving hearts
His new life will take root and increase

…may all hearts be filled with new life!

+ + +

Now Is the Hour

God's goodness is imprinted
Upon each person He creates
Yet He lets us choose for ourselves
The path of life we want to take

God's love extends this freedom
He watches so many turn away
How little we truly understand
This choice will bring loss our way

We lose our reverence for one another
Many people act in anger or hate
When disagreements bring adversity
Instead of listening we exaggerate

Enraged we become divided
Loathing only tears us apart
These matters need repair from within
They are conditions of the heart

Lord please shield all people
Help us be attentive to Your gaze
Your life in us will build up our faith
Please guard the goodness which You gave

Whatever is noble right and pure
Comes from You and Your abiding power
May we seize the moment
You have given us this day
Now is the hour

O

Open My Heart

Help me, Lord,
To want what you seek
To win hearts to you
From the greatest to the least

No agendas in mind
No scheme or plan
I want to open my heart
And give who I am

Increase in me
My trust in you
Help me spread your love
Through all I do

Our Assurance

Faith is not a guarantee
Goodness is all around
Faith is our assurance
God's love can always be found

God resides within all hearts
Be still and look within
When hope seems lost, God is calling
His love in us is where faith begins

+ + +

Our Hearts Must Unite

When we see the wrong that others do,
Our first reaction is to judge and condemn.
By doing that we avoid ourselves,
Because really we're no better than them.

We distract ourselves to keep sorrow away.
That inclination deprives us of life.
We must join together giving our burdens to God.
To conquer evil, our hearts must unite.

Our Own Beauty Is Passing

The mystery and the beauty
Within each person God creates
Is waiting to burst forth
Yet we question and hesitate

Christ dwells within each of us
Our divine beauty that is ever lasting
Do not be afraid to call Jesus friend
Because without Him
Our own beauty is passing

Let's celebrate our divine beauty!

P

Path of Life

God's goodness is imprinted
Upon each person He creates.
Yet He lets us choose for ourselves
The path of life we want to take.

God's love extends this freedom.
He watches so many turn away.
How little we truly understand
This choice brings harm our way.

Peace That Brings Rest

Darkness will never overcome
The light Christ offers to all.
Sickness, pain, and death itself,
Next to God becomes very small.

The goodness from God is the source of all power.
My prayer is for all to know.
His grace will one day rule the land.
But, first our hearts need to grow.

Surrendering ourselves is never easy.
We want to guard and protect.
But, this binds us to one another and the world.
Only God's love gives the peace that brings rest.

Please, Hold My Hand

Help me Lord,
To listen to You,
And to carry out,
What You desire.
Strengthen me,
And open my heart.
Set my life,
And soul, afire.
Your words impart,
Wisdom and glory,
And You ask us,
To partake.
I will drink,
From This Love,
So it dwells,
In me.
Please, hold my hand,
So I shall not forsake.

Power of Truth

Christ's love is gentle.
It will never coerce.
His truth brings power,
That is shared not forced.

May we carry out goodness,
For the glory of God.
His love bestows grace,
Where we struggle and trod.

Let us raise our actions
To this power of truth.
God will bestow blessings
On all that we do.

Praise Him

The Kingdom of God is not food or drink
Rather, it is righteousness and peace
Therefore, the purpose of our living is more
Than earning affection, money or things

God gives the strong something to run towards
And for the weak He will draw us near
Together, we must strive to live The Way
So God's Love is honored not feared

"Fear of the Lord" is our wonder
His awesome Love gives each of us life
May we praise Him today and always
Our love for God is what will end the word's strife

R

Reach Out

Why do we hide our loneliness?
It is in that very place we are in need.
When we sincerely open our hearts to one another,
God's love descends through you and me…

Reach out, and have a blessed day!

Receive Christ's Love

The Creator of our universe
Will never lead us astray
So, let the ray of your life's light
Shine in the darkness today

Praise the highest heavens
Give glory to God above
Be quick to give
And slow to take
In return
Receive Christ's love

Reflections of Grace

Grace is to our souls
What flowers are to Spring
God in all His mercy
To you His love He brings.

Christ renews our hope inside,
When the days seem long and dim.
He encourages and lifts the hearts
Of those who trust in Him.

Our Living God comes to us
Each and every day.
He embraces us with His love.
His grace shows us the way.

When our spirits are hurting
Christ will restore and bring new life.
Remain in Him because He promises,
His path for us is bright.

Reminders of Our Courage

Each of us is molded by our experiences,
Good and bad.
Remember, strength is manifested most
Through the struggles we have had.

Where there is injustice,
It is goodness we impart.
We might not always like it,
But peace is a matter of the heart.

We do not defend wrongdoing,
Nor can we forget our past.
We have reminders of our courage.
It is our fortitude that lasts.

+ + +

Rise Up

We are not justified
By the good things that we do.
Our worth comes from God,
Who created me and you.

Each of us is sacred
Because we are made in His image.
Together praising God,
We must rise up and pay Him homage.

Let us be blessings to one another today!

Run To Jesus

I cannot fix your wounded reality
Nor can you repair mine
We must remember whenever we're searching
Restoration comes from the Divine

Christ always gives us what we need
In faith we must surrender ourselves
Be intentional in this act of love
Trust in God and become your true self

Christ came to the world
He died on the cross
Then Jesus was laid in a tomb

He arose to new life
And raised us up too
Run to Jesus
He will heal all your wounds

65

S

Seed of Commitment

What is it that keeps nagging you
That shadow which darkens your heart
Perhaps it is an obsession or emotion
A desert that won't depart

It could be anger, worry, or sadness
Maybe confusion, resentment or fear
Whatever it is can be transformed
When our Mighty God is near

Those parts of ourselves that hold us back
Can become a seed of commitment
Faith, hope, and trust in God
Sheds light that enables persistence

Those seeming trials in our lives
Can help us thrive and achieve
God will lift our burdens and bless us
When we turn to Him and believe

What will you commit to today!

Seek God's Grace

We should turn to God with our weaknesses.
Let us not show pride.
His grace will rest upon us.
We no longer need to hide:

The anger we keep within ourselves…
Our selfishness and fears,
These things can be beaten,
When we know God's power is near.

God lifts the burdens of our sins,
Through Jesus Christ, our Lord.
Our weaknesses are made perfect.
Through His sacrifice, we are reborn.

Our pride becomes humility.
Our anger transforms to strength.
Our selfishness turns to love,
And our fears no longer have weight.

But, each one of us must seek God's hand.
He is with us every day.
Our Creator will never leave us.
He is with us to lead the way.

God's happiness is within us.
Through His grace we are fulfilled.
We must seek God's grace in all we do,
And know love will prevail.

Set Free

Lord,
In your embrace,
We are loved beyond measure,
And while living in this world
We will not be fully treasured.
Therefore, I must love others
The way that you love me.
We all want to know
We're cherished.
Through that
We are
Set Free.

Shadows

The shadows caused from our brokenness
Will distort and misalign
Yet, God looks at us and sees Himself
He knows we are made divine

Together, we are the Body of Christ
I need you and you need me
Each of us is a piece of this puzzle
Only together can we shine and be free

Shared Healing

We must never silence one another
Even when we don't agree
Let us be kind, listen and always forgive
Shared healing will come to you and me

Shine Bright

Stars are shining always,
But they require darkness to see their light
So it is with our hearts.
In the stillness is where they shine bright.

Special Graces

As Jesus' Mother,
Mary is always close to His heart.
That fact will make it natural
Special graces she will impart.

Let us not reject
This wondrous gift we have been given.
Our prayers joined with Mary's
Will help us get to heaven.

The salvation we seek
Comes from God alone.
But, we need one another
To find our way home.

Stoop

My freedom will never stop singing,
Even if I am bound by chains.
The laws of God are eternal,
So His goodness I will always proclaim.

God pours out His Love to all people.
He will never discriminate.
The good we receive depends on us.
Will I be thankful or will I hesitate?

When people demean one another,
It creates shame and doubt, never love.
Lord, I want to stoop with your grace
Help me offer your love from above.

The Choice Is Ours

We must surrender those parts of ourselves
That fill us with pain and sorrow.
Then grace from our Lord will send forth joy
With new life for a better tomorrow.

God is ever before us,
But the choice is ours to make.
When looking for lasting hope and love,
We must live our lives by faith.

The Dawn of How

We cannot achieve today
The things meant for tomorrow.
Time and lessons that are needed
Are impossible to borrow.

This moment is your gift.
Devote yourself to now.
Embrace what you've been given,
For it's the dawn of, "how"

How will tomorrow be?
That we do not know.
But, the seeds we sow today
Help us know that we will grow.

Growth brings wisdom and guarantees
We have all that we need.
Life is precious so be thankful!
The dawn of, "how" is…
Now indeed!

+ + +

The Goodness Within

It goes against my heart
To oppose your point of view.
Should I speak or be silent
I don't know what to do.

We so easily get offended
About things we've seen or heard.
Our souls are crying out,
And our hearts are being stirred.

The goodness within each of us
Must be united.
It's because of our fallen nature
That we have become divided.

Please be still and listen
To the One who loves you most.
Our Creator is the One
In whom we all should boast.

No person has the answer
And no law will fix our heart.
Only Goodness has the power
To bring light into the dark.

In my soul I'm praying for you.
God knows who you are.
God is always listening
To everyone, near and far.

The Hope of My Desires

Perfect in me oh Lord
Your divine grace
Beyond all telling

The hope of my desires
Dwells within
And is so compelling

THE POWER OF GOD
(Dedicated to those who are graduating)

It is time to move on,
And it's hard to ponder
The many things you have in store.
For it seems like just yesterday
You were babies for us to adore.

We still adore you, there is no doubt,
But now you've earned our esteem.
As a community of believers,
You are a vital part of our team.

Wherever you go, and whatever you do,
Consider the things you've been taught.
Our memories of you will remain.
You will never be far from our heart.

Move forward with strength,
And remember this day.
Keep love in your heart.
Don't forget to pray.

For the power of God is within you.
He will help you along your path,
And when temptations come along,
God will help you want good that will last.

We are all so very proud of you.
We send you forth with our blessing.
The light of Christ lives within you,
And God's love is everlasting.

The Ray of Your Life's Light

The conflicts and negative forces in our lives,
Come from the outside or from within.
When we place God at the center of our hearts,
His grace of restoration will begin.

We cannot escape the darkness.
Christ's light is needed in that place.
Let us be bold in loving.
We must join hearts and enter that space.

May the ray of your life's light
Shine in the darkness today.
Together, we must illumine all places
So evil has nowhere to prey.

Let your light shine!

Thrive

Lord, through our afflictions and crosses
We are sharing in Your crucified Love.
Come Holy Spirit and uphold all hearts.
We need your strength and grace from above.

Without You our world is such a dark place.
Help us listen so we can share in Your peace.
Show us how to serve the needs of others.
Yoked with Your Love our burdens are eased.

Humanity needs one another.
We all are struggling and must open our eyes.
May we never turn away from Your call.
Only together can we thrive and abide.

Through Christ We Are Reborn

God came to our world in human form.
He conquered death.
Through Christ we are reborn.

God has placed all life in our hands.
He gave us creation, all peoples, and lands.
His Love is ours. Hope is a gift too.
Faith, from our Lord helps us heed what is true.

As humans we're called to assist other's pain.
We will not heal when we seek selfish gain.
My heart hurts for the sufferings concealed.
I look for God's grace.
To His Love I will yield.

Together We'll Pray

How does God reach the depths of our souls
Predominately through our sufferings
And trials untold
While God doesn't send those things our way
He helps us navigate and provides joy for our day

God always pours out the love that we need
He bids forth His angels as we pray and plead
God never leaves us and is right by our side
The people who love us show how He abides
Spend some time with your Creator today
Look up to the heavens and together we'll pray

+ + +

Trust In God

I cannot fix your wounded reality.
Neither can you repair mine.
We all are lacking and always searching.
Our fulfillment comes from the Divine.

God always gives us what we need.
In faith we surrender ourselves.
Be intentional in this act of love.
Trust in God and find your true self.

Trust In His Love

There are times in my life when I feel weary.
I struggle and try, but cannot see clearly.
The happiness inside turns quickly to sorrow,
And I hope my tears become joy tomorrow.

My emotions feel raw. I become sad and dim.
I keep it hidden, but there is pain within.
During these times the Lord calls my name.
He wants to comfort, because He knows my pain.

The Mighty Physician offers grace that will heal.
He can cure me from the hurts I feel.
Our Lord has said He truly does care.
He won't force himself on me. I must turn to prayer.

I will look to God with thanksgiving and praise.
He offers His love, today and always.
I must listen to Him, that small voice inside.
The Lord is calling. He will help me abide.
Christ is my Lord. He gives strength from above.
Let go and let God. I must trust in His Love.

Tunnel of Darkness

Almighty God, we need Your help.
Our world is being oppressed.
We are in a tunnel of darkness,
Filled with doubt, fear, and loneliness.

Creator God, illumine our path.
Open our heart, so we can see.
Be our companion and dispel the shadows
Shed Your light, and pour down Your peace.

U

Unite Us Lord

God always uses
All things for His good.
As Christians we are called
To love as Christ would.

Do not be stirred
By dissention or wrong behavior.
Instead respond with grace,
And then call on your Savior.

Unite us Lord in our differences.
Please help our love increase.
We have become separated and torn.
Come Holy Spirit, pour out your peace.

+ + +

V

Victory

Arm us with your weapons Lord
Please come to our defense
Help us recognize the true enemy
Some are naïve to what we're up against

You guard and give us what we need
I'm obliged evil cannot hold You bound
Although shadows of death try to control and coerce
Our life in You is where victory will be found

W

Wake Up

Now is the time to stop and wake up.
Look around. Our world is hurting.
The Goodness within us must rise up.

Our love resists. We challenge and fight.
We want to prove, "You're wrong – I'm right."
God alone is faithful to all people and every need.
Wake up and look within.
Face your darkness. See your greed.

We get offended and stop listening.
Our hearts are closed and filled with spite.
We point fingers and blame others.
We are not God. Our love incites.

Let us commit to one another.
We must listen and join our hearts.
Our unique perspectives will not be helpful
If we use other's words to rip them apart.

Those people who do wrong.
Where were we when they needed our hand?
God's love will show us when we seek Him.
He helps us see and understand.

Now is the time to stop and wake up.
Look around. Our world is hurting.
The goodness within us must rise up.

Look around you ♥ who needs your hand today

+ + +

Walking Side by Side

Each of us is compelled to act
When wrongs need to be made right
What you and I are called to do,
Will be different so we must not fight

The goodness in you is always right
And the goodness in me is right too
Walking side by side one another
Our goodness grows and will lead us through

Want What Is Good

When my selfish heart yields
And it is for others I want what is good
I know God is at work in me
And I am acting as I should

We All Belong

When we hold others to their past,
How does mercy begin?
We won't recognize repentance,
If we keep holding up their sins.

We must be careful of the things we say.
Our pride will fool and divide.
Let us hold fast to God and His love.
In Him we are called to reside.

Goodness will always enlighten.
A change of heart ought to begin.
Let us never judge another.
God surely knows all our sins.

Together let us love and learn.
We are called to know right from wrong.
God's freedom and justice will unite us all.
To Him we all belong.

We Must Be Active

Darkness and evil are perilous.
With no light the truth remains hidden.
It will persuade uncertainty and illusions.
People will doubt and become fearfully ridden.

It is powerful and wishes to engulf our world.
So we must be active against this gloom.
Let us humbly surrender ourselves to God.
His enlightenment will cast out all doom.

We Need One Another

God, you are carrying each of us.
So, I put my trust in you today.
We need your love because ours always finds fault.
Help us serve justice and goodness always.

Your mercy will bestow liberty.
Without You life on earth has no peace.
We may divide ourselves but we need one another
Lord, may all hope in you be released.

What Is Holding You Back

Do you know what is holding you back?
We all suffer many hurts from within.
Holy Spirit please come to our aide.
Dwell in all hearts – let your healing begin.

Lord, give me grace to take a risk,
Although I may be misunderstood.
I want to impart Your knowledge and Word,
Offering truth and all that is good.

When we desire lasting peace in our world
And sincerely want unity to grow.
We must remember when praying for others
To lift up our friends and our foes.

When Jesus Left

When Jesus left His apostles
They were scared and so confused
Those same experiences in our own lives
Leave us uncertain what we're called to do

Help me Lord to enter Your rest
Some days are so easy but others are a test
I know the good I want to do
Yet so often I can't seem to follow through

Each new day please help me recall
The Holy Spirit remains
And provides grace for us all

Where Peace Resides

I will not run after one chasing the world,
So as not to grow weary and tired.
Instead, I will cling to my God and Savior.
His Holy Spirit assures to inspire.

I cannot become distracted,
Or forget the war has been won.
Life's battles must never drive me,
Lest within Christ's work is undone.

Rather, I trust in prayer to the Lord.
It's in Him truth and light remain.
Christ conquered darkness once and for all.
His love and goodness are here to stay.

Therefore, I
Shall not run nor hide.
I will stand with Christ,
Where peace resides.

Will Goodness

Are you listening to your heart?
Goodwill towards all dwells within.
Will goodness for those who have wronged you?
That is how the drumbeat of peace begins.

For some this can be a challenge.
Many others will simply refuse.
Be freed from the chains that bind and hate?
The pulse of grace is what we must choose.

Y

You and Me

I will not defend wrongdoing,
From Democrats, Republicans, or anyone else.
I want to endorse goodness,
And I suspect so does everyone else.

Election campaigns can be alarming.
Some are sad and mind-boggling too.
Many shrink without even thinking,
Dishonoring what is noble and true.

We must decide right now
To look within our own heart.
Where can I make a difference?
In that place is where I should start.

Our unified trust in kindness
Will be seen through our good deeds.
Candidates will make more laws.
Lasting love comes from you and me.

You Love Me

This road I am traveling is a lonely one indeed.
It leaves me feeling sad, in such a state of need.
Thank you for not scorning me, Lord.

I know You love me so.
Your assurance helps me open my heart.
You give me hope so I can grow.

You Will Never Be the Same

All souls are united,
Through a God we cannot see.
His love pours out, to all the world.
It's freely given to you and me.

Your soul knows his goodness.
You were fashioned then set free.
God longs for your return.
Friendship with God is meant to be.

When you are seeking fulfillment,
Listen for his voice, and call out his name.
In the silence, you will find him.
You will never be the same.

+ + +

+ + +

Part Two
Christmas Poems

Christmastime
(Christmas 2006)

Shopping lists and carols
Remind us Christmas is almost here.
Reindeer, wreaths, and snowmen
Will fill our hearts with cheer.

Christmastime brings memories
Of music, gifts, and more.
We decorate our homes
And meet loved ones at our door.

Take a moment to reflect
The Christmastimes gone-by.
So much can be forgotten
Unless we call to mind.

Grandma's house and Santa Claus
Delight the hearts of many.
Children filled with wonder
Help make cookies and homemade candy.

As days go by and time brings change,
It's not easy to let go.
That's when our faith must lead us.
Acknowledge God is in control.

+ + +

At Christmastime we celebrate
The Creator of all things.
We extol and honor Jesus Christ,
Because He is our King.

All glory goes to our God on high.
Let us offer thanksgiving and praise.
He will bestow upon us hope
On Christmas and all our days.

Be still and listen at Christmastime
To the very small voice inside.
The Lord is calling each of us,
And He will help us to abide.

Christ is close within each heart.
He offers us strength from above.
This Christmastime let go and let God.
Receive the gift that is love.

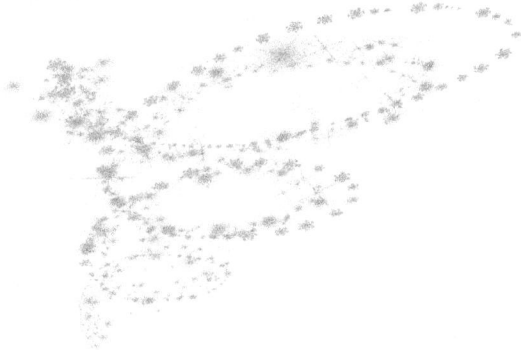

Treasured Gifts
(Christmas 2007)

We have so many treasured gifts.
Family and friends top the list.
Our homes we can surely be thankful for,
The food we eat, and so much more.

This time of year brings to mind
That giving gifts is something kind.
So we think of others and want to share.
What can I give to show I care?

We're busy buying
And soon become stressed.
We want to slow down
But cannot resist.

There's so much to do
And so little time.
We keep spending money
And standing in lines.

We soon become tired
And need some rest.
Each day it grows harder
To be our best.

Stop. Slowdown.
Be still. Look above.
The greatest gift
Of all is love.

With the gift of love come other gifts too,
Such as joy…and hope…and gratitude.
Give the gift of yourself – be gentle and true.
Encourage one another in all that you do.

The gift of understanding
Shows courage and faith.
Be thoughtful and nice
Each day that you wake.

Your patience and peace
Shows others you care.
These are gifts you can give
If only you dare.

These gifts are special
And treasured indeed.
We long for love –
We all are in need.

These gifts are free,
But they came at a price.
Jesus Christ was born
And then sacrificed.

He gave his life
So that we might live,
And share treasured gifts.
They're our gifts to give.

+ + +

Awaken Your Joy!
(Christmas 2008)

This time of year
As I sit and ponder
The things I am grateful for,
I remember you
And give thanks to God.
Our world offers much to adore.

Although these times are trying
And the economy is not the best,
Our God is with us always
Assuring and giving us rest.

The earth with all its beauty,
God's handiwork abounds.
His love for us is infinite.
Just take a look around.

All things in life
From the small to the grand,
Flourish and prosper
In the palm of God's hand.

The warmth of God's love
Is calming indeed.
Go and share His love,
Because we all are in need.

+ + +

The power of love,
With its sanctifying grace,
Will lead us to hope
And fill us with faith.

With faith we can know
That within us God dwells.
It reminds us to trust
And know all will be well.

We are children of God
Filled with hope and delight.
Awaken Your Joy!
Dwell not on your plight.

Peace on earth is our wish.
What a wonderful thing.
Keep God in your heart
So the whole world can sing.

Petition, praise, thanksgiving,
Go to God with your prayers.
Intercede for one another
And pray because you care

+ + +

Hope Presents...
(Christmas 2009)

Hope has many faces,
It dwells within each heart,
It's put there to instruct,
And given to impart...

May the Hope within,
That comes from above,
Be awakened through grace,
And ignited with love...

Rekindle the Hope,
Of days gone by,
You have nothing to lose,
Unless you don't try...

God made our hearts,
To be a wonderful place,
Overflowing with Hope,
And filled with His grace...

Encouragement and commitment,
These gifts go hand in hand,
God gives us Hope and purpose,
They are part of His great plan...

+ + +

Angel of God,
Be with me today,
Help me to Hope,
And remind me to pray...

I must put my best foot forward,
That is all I have to do,
Possibilities await us,
It is up to me and you...

Hope is always on our side,
It's a gift for us to use,
Hope tells of God's eternal love,
A truth we can't refuse...

Jesus bestowed upon us Hope,
When he came to the earth from above,
This Hope presents God's greatest gift...
UNCONDITIONAL LOVE

Where You Are
(Christmas 2010)

Long ago His voice rang out,
And our world came into being.
He still whispers and reveals Himself
Within the beauty of everything.

He gives His peace and harmony
And sustains you through the day.
Make sure you watch and listen.
He is never far away.

Be still and pay attention.
He will show Himself to you.
Will you recognize Him?
He is there in all you do.

His love is pure and simple.
Truly something to hold dear,
And that is why we celebrate
This special time of year.

Jesus is our Lord of life.
Hear Him calling out your name…
In the winds of the summertime,
And in the pouring of the rain.

During long cold days of winter,
You have reasons to rejoice.
For, in silence and in darkness,
He is always very close.

His gift of love will warm your heart.
You need not look too far.
Jesus Christ is beside you now.
He is with you where you are!

+ + +

PRECIOUS MOMENTS
(Christmas 2011)

Time is a treasured gift.
It's more prized than any gold.
God gives it to inspire
For the young…and for the old.

The times that are enduring,
Precious moments to behold,
Are God's most valued gifts to us…
The recollections of the soul.

Recall a special memory
When true love touched your heart.
This wonder you were given
Is a gift God did impart.

Compassion, joy & kindness…
God's love is all around.
We grow and are most happy
Where heaven on earth is found.

A holy day dawned upon us
That night when Christ was born,
And now we celebrate each year
As humanity is transformed.

For when time was created
Christ commanded all to be,
And because of His great love for us
He died for you and me.

But time could not contain Him
Nor death could have its way,
And through Christ's resurrection…
His Spirit is here to stay.

The angels with all creation
Know God's love is everlasting.
Eternity comes from above
While on earth our time is passing.

The faith and love we need so much
Are moments that will last,
And the miracle of miracles…
When all good will come to pass.

So give of yourself to others,
Precious moments of your time.
You will discover what is lasting,
And eternity you will find.

The Way
(Christmas 2012)

Jesus came into our world
To show us The Way.
He taught us how to find peace
When we're filled with dismay.
Christ traveled the road
Of compassion and love.
In Him we have hope,
Through His grace from above.
Our world is so broken.
It is in such need.
We must do our part.
Let us all take heed...

"I'll be mindful of my sinfulness,
And although it does not cause
All the suffering that I see,
It's still helpful to take pause;
The consequences
Of my sins will reflect.
'What are my sins?'
We may ask.
It's wrongdoing I neglect."

When we turn to our Savior,
He will forgive all our sins.
We then reflect our Lord,
And God's healing begins.
God's inheritance of peace
Then dwells within,
And no one can take it away.
This gift grants freedom,
It is given for all.
Follow Christ.
He will show you the way

The Giver of Gifts
(Christmas 2013)

Jesus is the giver of gifts.
In him all good is foreseen.
With hope we await the dawn of our Lord.
Through Christ comes our destiny.
Sustained by the gifts God gives to the world,
We are led by his Spirit to know;
The splendor of seven wonderful gifts
That enable our spirits to grow.

The first and most perfect gift
Tells the value of persons and things.
This gift is called **Wisdom**,
Which helps us discern.
In truth, all insight she brings.

Understanding is another gift.
Appreciation and hope it imparts.
Through understanding we gain conviction of faith
And beliefs that will live in our hearts.

Another gift is **Counsel**,
Which helps us know how to proceed.
With it we learn sincerity and trust.
Right Judgment will teach honesty.

Courage is granted by our lord
As a gift that instills inner strength.
Fortitude brings true peace to our life.
Confidence in God helps our worries abate.

+ + +

By **Knowledge** we're aware of temptations
And know what God wants from our lives.
We're attentive to do what is good for us
And can live our life's purpose and thrive.

Reverence increases our love for God.
It gives respect for earth and all life.
In **Piety** we learn generosity of heart,
And want to do what is right.

Wonder and awe is called **Fear of the Lord**
And helps us know how to respond.
This gift will call us to celebrate
And grasp how we depend on God.

Jesus is the giver of gifts,
So be watchful throughout your days.
His Spirit will pour out these gifts to us,
Always, and in all ways.

Gifts of the Holy Spirit
Wisdom
Understanding
Council (or Right Judgement)
Fortitude (or Courage)
Knowledge
Piety (or Reverence)
Fear of the Lord (or Wonder and Awe)

BELIEVE
(Christmas 2014)

There is a knowing
In my soul,
Of something great
Beyond measure.
And the stirrings
Of my heart,
Come from Love,
Christ's true treasure.

God, Our Father,
Sent Jesus,
To enlighten.
I must look
Inside myself.
Do I doubt?
Am I frightened?

This time I have
On earth,
Can seem
A great divide.
I shall search
For our Lord,
With trust.
By faith
I will not hide.

+ + +

In the desert,
Of my life,
I will build
An oasis of Love.
The Holy Spirit
Of heaven and earth,
Extends His graces
From above.

I will seek
What is good,
Know God's truth,
And follow His call.
Be bold,
~Believe~
And pray!
Christ's Love
Is meant for all!

Merry Christmas

+ + +

Holiness Is Calling!
(Christmas 2015)

In that sacred moment
When Jesus Christ was born
God's mercy came into the world
For the weary and the torn

Let us reconcile divisions
Be inspired with grateful hearts
By the power of the Holy Spirit
Know the King of kings imparts

Fruits of the Holy Spirit
Perfections formed in us
They reflect God's eternal glory
Revealing obedience and trust

Each of us is a child of God
We're created by His love
Charity is our mission
With a calling from above

God's supernatural life
Will lead us to His grace
His joy it will bestow
And make known the gift of faith

We must celebrate God's Peace
In our everyday living
Our trust in God's will
A cause for praise and thanksgiving

Patience is a loving witness
It is something we should enfold
Having forbearance in each situation
Is an ideal to uphold

+ + +

We are asked to spread God's Kindness
Jesus calls us to forgive
Let us be an example to others
Of how we ought to live

Nourish yourself with Goodness
Fill your heart with glory and praise
God's Generosity will follow
When you live your life this way

Gentleness and Faithfulness
These things go hand in hand
God transforms our souls to greatness
Because it's part of His vast plan

Modesty and Self-Control
Reveal humility from above
God's promise of salvation
Is found from this great love

Know the gift of who you are
Show your beauty and purity of life
Selfless love calls us to Chastity
We must always, "Put on Christ"

Holiness is calling!
Let us take a look around
God's love for us is infinite
Through Christ we're heaven bound

The Fruits of the Holy Spirit are:
Charity, Joy, Peace, Patience, Forbearance, Kindness, Goodness,
Generosity, Gentleness, Faithfulness, Self-Control, and Chastity.

+ + +

Proclaim Jesus
(Christmas 2016)

God came into our world as a child
Quietly, one holy night.
The lonesome road Mary and Joseph trod,
Paved the way for doing what's right.

That same obedience calls you and me.
Grace will always lead the way.
Give glory to God in all that is good,
Through the things you do and say.

Life, and all its beauty,
Will lead you to the gift of faith.
Our Lord consoles and brings healing,
Where there is strife, cruelty or hate.

Recall what is truthful and ponder.
Do your attitudes hold you bound?
God always extends his mercy,
So heaven on earth can be found.

God longs to give his love to you.
That's why Christ was born on earth.
Be still and open your heart.
His life in you will awaken new birth.

Christ's affection for you is eternal.
He is with you through creation and time.
His laws will make your joy complete.
Always strive to be of one mind.

View your soul as a reflection
Of the ponderings in your heart.
Do you call on the Holy Spirit?
Faith, hope and love He will impart.

Do nothing with selfish ambition.
Shine with the innocence of God the Son.
Proclaim Jesus, your brother and friend.
Only through Him can heaven be won.

+ + +

Within Your Heart
(Christmas 2017)

Do you know
The Living Christ
The Lord of Creation
Whose breath gives you life?

His Love for you
Is so profound
It is our meagerness that straps
This Mighty Love bound

We must humble ourselves
To have peace on earth
Jesus came into our world
Preparing the earth for rebirth

We are unable to understand
God's vast mysterious ways
So in our human tenderness
We wander and go astray

The complexities of our connectedness
Cannot be seen or touched
It is through God's miraculous Divinity
We are united and lifted up

Keep in mind no one can take it from you
Nor can anyone take it from me
That gift God personally gives each of us
His Divine Love, which will set you free

So, when we see misplaced pride in others
May we grow and become aware of our own
For within your heart, and within every heart
Is where God desires to be at home

*May your heart and home be filled with Jesus' Life and Peace
during this Holy Season, and always!*

Christ's Gift of Love
(Christmas 2018)

God has come into the world
Your Creator you can personally know
Blessed are those who seek the Lord
Christ's friendship brings peace to the soul

When your longing heart meets God
Your desires and wants are met
Take time to receive Christ's gift of love
Certainty of hope is what His love begets

God formed the universe out of nothing
Through His intimacy your divine nature was made
Christ's light within you wants to shine brightly
Will you share it without being afraid?

Deep within you God is dwelling
Quietly offering grace, He calls out your name
In contrast, the world and all its glamour
Shouts out power, fortune, and fame

The world's things are impressive and luring
But they do not bestow devotion
You may obtain but will always want more
Until one day you're just going through motions

Sincerely we must turn towards one another
Christ's humble love will open our hearts
The Holy Spirit is here to enlighten us
God's grace He will readily impart

Humanity aids God in creation
Just as through Mary, Jesus was born
So too with us, heaven sings with joy
When Christ's life in us is embraced and adored

Christ's gift of love is what we are celebrating
It is through Jesus all goodness is won
Have courage and faithfully honor Him
It is our "Yes" that makes hearts beat as one

SHINE BRIGHT
(Christmas 2019)

Stars are shining always
But they require darkness to see their light
So it is with our hearts
In stillness is where they shine bright

The shadows caused from our brokenness
Distort the light and misalign
Yet God looks at us and sees Himself
He knows we are made divine

Standing together with one another
All in need and all with scars
Each of us is a child of God
We have been chosen from near and far

Together we are the Body of Christ
I need you and you need me
Each person is a piece of this puzzle
Only together will we glow and be free

Grace is what will free us
It heals our wounds and sooths our pain
It guards our dignity and leads to hope
Our light is ignited for glory and praise

Grace will not restrict us
It is hidden yet comes from Love
We are provided all things needed
But we must turn to our God above

At odds with so many
We turn away and then we fret
That does not solve our problems
Or resolve the world's regrets

+ + +

If only we all knew
What lies deep within each soul
We would take heed and be awakened
God's Love in the world would grow

That reservation put in all hearts
Is meant for Christ alone
It was placed there by God
To shine bright and welcome us home

www.ingramcontent.com/pod-product-compliance
Lightning Source LLC
Chambersburg PA
CBHW021133020426
42331CB00005B/745